tECHiES™

Linus Torvalds

Linus Torvalds

{ Software Rebel }

ANN BRASHARES

TWENTY-FIRST CENTURY BOOKS
BROOKFIELD, CONNECTICUT

Special thanks to Bradley Wellington for contributing "Tech Talk"

Design by Lynne Amft

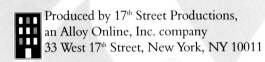 Produced by 17th Street Productions,
an Alloy Online, Inc. company
33 West 17th Street, New York, NY 10011

Library of Congress Cataloging-in-Publication Data

Brashares, Ann.
  Linus Torvalds : software rebel / Ann Brashares.
       p. cm.— (Techies)
  Includes index.
  ISBN 0-7613-1960-3 (lib. bdg.)
   1. Torvalds, Linus, 1969—Juvenile literature. 2. Computer programmers—Finland—
Biography—Juvenile literature. 3. Linux—Juvenile literature. [1. Torvalds, Linus, 1969-
2. Computer programmers. 3. Linux. 4. Computer software industry.] I. Title. II. Series.

QA76.2.S7 B73 2001
005.1'092—dc21
[B]
                                      00-066791

contents

CHAPTER ONE

Changing the Future

The Most Famous Computer Programmer in the World

WHO IS THE MOST FAMOUS COMPUTER PROGRAMMER IN THE WORLD?

BILL GATES, YOU MIGHT ANSWER, AND YOU WOULD BE PARTLY RIGHT. BUT ALTHOUGH GATES STARTED HIS CAREER AS A PROGRAMMER, HE ACHIEVED FAME AND FORTUNE AS A BUSINESSMAN AND A MARKETER—NOT A TECHNICIAN.

WHO IS THE MOST FAMOUS COMPUTER PROGRAMMER IN THE WORLD?

If you put this question to a techie crowd, chances are you would get one single resounding answer: Linus Torvalds. He has more listings on the World Wide Web than Steve Jobs, Bill Gates, Larry Ellison, and even Tom Cruise.

Linus who?

Okay, so he is not a household name. He is not a multibillionaire. He does not own a jet. He has never brought a company public in a soaring initial public offering (IPO) like many of the techies you have probably heard of.

But that is what makes Linus Torvalds so special. He is often called the anti–Bill Gates. He has not made any money from his software, although he has practically created a revolution. He wrote an operating system called Linux, a widely admired platform that competes with Windows. And this is the amazing part: He gives it away *for free*. Yes, free. You and anyone else on the planet with a computer, a modem, and a decent amount of space on your hard drive can download it from the Internet.

You may not have heard of him, but you can bet that Bill Gates has. Torvalds is not making any money from Linux, but he is changing the way software is written, updated, and

Linus Torvalds proudly holds a license plate bearing the "Linux" name.

distributed. And he is making a lot of people wonder why they should pay for Windows or any other expensive system when they can get Linux for nothing.

Even more important, Torvalds has been instrumental in creating a thriving community. He has invited every Linux user and programmer to help him write the code and eradicate the bugs to make Linux better. Linux is the brainchild of one great programmer, but it is the product of millions.

So, although Linus Torvalds may not be a household name . . . *yet* . . . he has made software free, he has made it inclusive, he has made it adaptable, and while he was at it, he changed the future of computing.

A Strong and Independent Mind

Linus (pronounced LEE-nuss) Benedict Torvalds was born in Helsinki, the capital of Finland, on December 28, 1969. According to legend, he was named both for Linus Pauling,

Dr. Linus Pauling, winner of the Nobel Prize for chemistry and peace

Helsinski, Finland—Linus's hometown

the chemist, and for the blanket-toting Peanuts character. His family was among a minority population of Swedish-speaking Finns, known as *finlandssvensk*. Although native Swedish speakers in Finland account for only 6 percent of the population, Swedish is counted (along with Finnish) as one of Finland's two official languages.

According to his father, Nils Torvalds, his son's strong and independent mind was well apparent by the time he was eight years old. "On Christmas, I gave him a fairly complicated model ship and thought that we in a father-and-son-together

A model ship like the one Linus built—by himself—when he was eight years old

way would build it. The following morning, he had already made it all by himself," his father recounted.

Torvalds became fascinated by computers at the age of ten. "What else are you going to do in Finland if you hate ice hockey?" he jokes. His grandfather, Leo Toerngvist, a professor of statistics at the University of Helsinki, brought home one of the very early personal computers, a Commodore VIC-20, and encouraged Torvalds to use it. "I started programming because you had to make it work," Torvalds remembers. Within a short time, young Torvalds was writing his own computer games.

From that point on, programming became his passion and his obsession. Although his father tried to get him interested in sports, it did not work. "I was never very good," Torvalds says now.

As a child, he was disciplined and single-minded, but not dogmatic. "He once said that he won't eat sweets," his father recounted. "I promised him one hundred Finnish marks if he kept that promise for a year. He did, but the following day [after the bet was completed], he took the money and bought sweets for the whole sum."

It is that very combination of dedication and pragmatism that has put him at the center of a great technological upheaval: the open-source code movement.

The Good Old Days of Free Software

Torvalds was not the first computer programmer to feel that software should not be owned or controlled, that it should be available freely to everybody. In fact, up until the 1980s, nobody really thought of software as something to sell on a grand scale at all. It was not so much idealism that made software free back then. Programmers did not have the sense they were giving away anything of great potential value. Hardware—the stuff you could touch, type on, see—that was considered the real product. That's what engineers and businesspeople believed you made money on. Software was sort of a necessary evil to make your hardware useful.

In many ways, this was a more idealistic and innocent time,

Microsoft offices in Redmond, Washington.
The company kick-started the software revolution.

before people thought to control software and make a bundle on it. A great number of computer scientists and programmers look back on this time with longing. There was an open, scholarly atmosphere of experimentation and risk-taking among the early computer professionals and hobbyists. They represented a small, prescient minority, and to a large degree they stuck together to support their fledgling technology.

The early personal-computer hobbyists habitually copied and passed around software without much thought to copyrights and licenses. The now-famous Homebrew Computer Club in Menlo Park, California, stands as the epitome of that old spirit. (Among its faithful were Steve Wozniak and Steve Jobs, founders of Apple Computers, as well as many other computer visionaries.) The Homebrew was the premier place for obtaining or sharing any piece of software making the rounds. And ironically, it was there that many people claim the age of free software officially came to an end.

The Information Age

In 1976, Bill Gates was a very young, very recent college dropout. He was struggling to legitimize his new company—Micro-soft, as it was written then—and was chagrined to discover his new software was making the rounds at the Homebrew. Gates did not take it lightly. He responded with his angry "Open Letter to Hobbyists."

"Most of you steal your software," Gates accused the Homebrew faithful. "One thing you do . . . is prevent good software from being written. Who can afford to do professional work for nothing?" To the old-timers it was like Eve crunching on the apple, bringing the age of innocence to an end. It introduced a new consciousness that ideas were not necessarily to be shared, and they certainly were not free.

That great blue-chip computer giant, IBM, was the company most famously caught off-guard thinking of software the old-fashioned way. They made at least two critical oversights that cost them a few hundred billion dollars and helped mint the two richest men in the world—Bill Gates of Microsoft, of course, and Larry Ellison of Oracle.

IBM's first tough lesson came in 1981 at the hands of Bill Gates. That was the year they gave Microsoft the license to provide the operating system—MS-DOS—that came on their brand-new personal computers. But they did not require exclusivity from Microsoft—in other words, they did not ask that Microsoft not sell that same software to anybody else. Microsoft sold the very same software to a flock of brand-new IBM competitors, and suddenly IBM had no edge in the

Software giant: Larry Ellison of Oracle

hardware market. IBM was not the standard, as they had hoped they would be. Microsoft was.

This sent a revelation like a lightning bolt through the computer industry. The future was not in hardware; it was in software. Anybody could make a plastic box containing the right chip for a few pennies less. Software was the proprietary, unique product—the *intellectual* property. This revelation marked a major milestone in what we now call "the information age." People began to understand the value of ideas. They recognized that things you can't necessarily touch or feel—software, music, movies, novels, poems, articles, games—are ultimately more valuable than things you can. But intellectual property is notoriously hard to contain. It is a lot easier to lay claim to your mountain bike, say, than to your ideas.

IBM's second oversight came in the mid-1980s. Top-level IBM scientists wrote and released papers on how to write something called a relational database. A relational database is a software system that allows you to sort through a huge ocean of information in exactly the way you choose. Say your relational database contains information on every baseball game ever played. You can ask it to tell you exactly which no-hitters were pitched in Kansas in the 1970s when the temperature fell below 40°F (4.4°C), and it will (if there were any such games). The search engines we use online depend on this technology. In fact, the relational database, as much as any other technology, has made the Internet what it is today. IBM scientists figured out how to write this software, but it was Larry Ellison's company, Oracle, that made billions selling it. Why? Because IBM did not even think to keep these ideas secret. They published a virtual blueprint for the database in academic papers meant to be part of a larger dialogue among computer scientists. You did not *own* these sorts of ideas. You did not sell them. Or so they thought.

The 1980s and 1990s represent a more cynical time, when aggressive, gargantuan companies such as Microsoft came to control the software on more than 85 percent of the computers in the world and made it extremely difficult for small companies to compete. (So much so that the U.S. government brought a massive lawsuit against Microsoft, claiming that Microsoft competed unfairly . . . but that's another story altogether.)

And yet the new millennium seems to be witnessing another fundamental shift back to the free flow of ideas. In part the shift is due to the Internet. Its instantaneous, free distribution of any and all intellectual property makes it *very* difficult to control the flow of information. In fact, some people believe the Internet will spell the end of copyright—of legal and practical ownership of ideas. In part the shift is due to Linus Torvalds and other idealistic programmers (or simply practical ones, as Torvalds would argue), who have reawakened the spirit of free software. Now the free software movement is growing and strengthening across the globe. Some people even believe the free software movement will topple the software giants in time.

CHAPTER TWO

The Birth of Linux

How It Started

WHEN LINUS TORVALDS WAS IN HIS SECOND YEAR AT HELSINKI UNIVERSITY IN 1990, HE DECIDED TO BUY A NEW COMPUTER. ALTHOUGH HE'D GOTTEN HIS START ON HIS GRANDFATHER'S COMMODORE AT HOME, HE'D SPENT TIME AT THE UNIVERSITY WORKING ON MAINFRAME COMPUTERS RUNNING AN OPERATING SYSTEM CALLED UNIX. AN OPERATING SYSTEM (OS) IS LIKE THE CENTRAL NERVOUS SYSTEM OF THE COMPUTER. IT COMMUNICATES BETWEEN THE HARDWARE AND THE SOFTWARE APPLICATIONS AND CREATES THE COMPUTING environment. Software applications—games, word-processing systems, spreadsheets, browsers—run on top of a computer's operating system.

Torvalds liked the personal computers running Intel's widely used 386 chip, but all of them came with Microsoft's DOS operating system. "I knew I didn't want DOS," Torvalds explained. "I'd seen DOS." He wanted to buy a version of Unix, but it was far too expensive, and it was not made to run on a PC.

So what did he do? "I decided to make my own Unix," Torvalds explained. "What do I need? I need lots of ignorance, because if you know too much, you know that it's obviously impossible. Then you need the arrogance—'yes, I can do it, and I can do it better than anybody else.' Those two you need just to get started . . . you need to be a bit crazy and actually go on with it."

At first he just wanted to write enough software to enable his computer to do the basic tasks he needed. He began by writing code to allow the various pieces of hardware—

Linus Torvalds spreads the word about Linux.

computer, monitor, disk drives—to communicate. Then he developed a filing system and kept going from there. "I noticed that this was starting to be an operating system," he said. He borrowed ideas from a system called Minix, a miniature, simplified version used for teaching Unix, and used them as an armature for his fledgling system. But soon he had replaced all the Minix code with code more perfectly suited to his own needs.

"Forget about dating! Forget about hobbies! Forget about life," Torvalds says of that time in his life. "We are talking about a guy who sat, ate, and slept in front of the computer."

In the fall of 1991, at the age of twenty-one, he put his operating system, Linux (pronounced LINN-ucks) version 0.01, on the Internet and told some people about it. He not only released the system itself; he also released what is called the source code—the underlying instructions used to create the software. Seeing the source code allows other programmers to access exactly how the writer did what he did. This kind of open or accessible source code also allows people other than the original writer to fix the software, to alter it to suit their own needs, or even to distribute it to other users and programmers. This is why Linux is called an open-source code system, as opposed to Windows or other proprietary software, in which the source code is closed or hidden—

unavailable to the wider community of programmers for fixes or alterations. Because Torvalds did not charge anybody any money for it, it joined the library of free software called freeware.

Originally he chose the name Freix (the -*ix* from Unix). It was meant to be sort of a silly pun. "But it turns out that the person who had the FTP site* in Finland didn't like the 'Freix' part, so he just decided on Linux instead," Torvalds remembers.

"The first thing I got was a lot of comments," Torvalds said. And he responded to those comments, making the system bigger and better. Soon after that, users not only e-mailed him suggested improvements but began e-mailing him code— actual patches of programming to fix a bug or adapt the system to a new use. If Torvalds felt the patch was useful and well executed, he would apply it to the larger system. In the beginning he was getting comments and code from about five to ten

*FTP stands for "file transfer protocol." An FTP site is a public-access Web site for posting and downloading files.

people, and then the number of contributors began to grow. "It got better and better," Torvalds says of baby Linux.

Torvalds coordinated the efforts of this growing number of developers, making sure the system continued to improve and to grow in a healthy and coherent way. He released subsequent versions, .02, .03, and .04, responding quickly to the improvements of his collaborators.

"Copyleft"

To make sure the Linux source code stayed open and the software free, Torvalds formally released the operating system under a license known as "copyleft," pioneered by the free software crusader Richard Stallman, founder of the Free Software Foundation, based in Cambridge, Massachusetts. "Copyleft" (as opposed to the traditional copyright, in which a person legally secures ownership of his or her work) means that the software can be copied and altered and distributed any number of times, but the source code must always remain open and accessible to all. Torvalds wanted to be sure that no matter what personal or professional decision he or the other developers made in their lives, none of them could own Linux—nobody could sell it to Microsoft or bury the source code. "I wanted people to be able to trust me without trusting me personally," Torvalds said. "So even if I turn to the dark side, nobody can take it over."

As Linux grew and more programmers contributed substantial pieces beyond the basic kernel or core of the system, Torvalds encouraged them to issue similar licenses in their own names, so now there are many licensers of Linux. "Nobody can fundamentally change it now because they'd have to coordinate everybody who owns these pieces," Torvalds explains.

It is not a decision he has ever regretted. "When it comes to Linux," he says, "the one decision I am most proud of is not the actual physical design of the system, but the decision to make it free."

Linux 1.0 (and Counting)

In March 1994, Torvalds released Linux 1.0—once again over the Internet—signifying the first stable, complete version of the system. Although Linux already had more than 100,000 users, Torvalds resisted calling a version 1.0 until it had a proper networking capability, allowing computers to connect easily to one another. So at last, three years after the project began, it had every essential component of a true operating system.

The number of users and codevelopers grew at a dizzying rate, and still Torvalds managed to run the vast network from a small apartment in Helsinki he shared with his then girlfriend (now wife) Tove, the six-time karate champion of Finland. Word of Linux was beginning to spread beyond its circle of devotees, and soft-spoken Torvalds was fast becoming a programming legend. Yet he remained a graduate student at the University of Helsinki and collected a modest stipend. The university allowed him to devote almost all his time to Linux, and the Linux community helped him pay off

Jon Hall, executive director of Linux International, plays with a live penguin.

Parading penguins—the inspiration for the Linux logo

his debt on the computer he used at home for Linux development.

When people questioned why this technical visionary would remain a poor student in Finland instead of getting a "real job," he responded, "I've been very happy with this arrangement—I get to do whatever I want, and I have no commercial pressures whatsoever doing this. . . . As I've been able to live happily on university pay, the deciding factor is not so much the money as the interest level of any 'real job' (but lest somebody gets the idea that money doesn't matter at all, I'll just mention that yes, it does)."

In June 1996, after many intermediary versions, Torvalds released version 2.0, which offered users the ability to run the Linux platform on a wider variety of computers—those using chips other than the Intel x86 family, for example, or computers powered by more than one microprocessor.

By this time, Linux users constituted a fanatical code-writing army. The project grew so rapidly, with so much harnessed brainpower, that Torvalds's own code shrank to a small minority. He estimates that at least 90 percent of the Linux code is written by others. While his original release was 10,000 lines of code—all of which have since been rewritten—Linux now has about 15 million lines.

The Linux troops decided they needed a logo, so the choice was given to Torvalds. He chose a penguin. Why? "Partly accident, partly because I like penguins," he explains. "Partly because I was bitten by a penguin. It was at an open zoo. I made my finger look like a herring—and the penguin fell for it. It was a very, very timid bite." Some of the Linux faithful complained the logo was not serious or high-tech enough, but Torvalds disagrees. "I'm much happier being associated with a fun and slightly irreverent logo than with something static and boring."

Yes, Linux Is Free, But Is It Good?

On the whole, Linux has been adopted by a more technologically sophisticated group of users than Windows or Macintosh. Linux is not as user-friendly as those platforms (not yet, anyway), and it does not have the large and complex overlays to make the computing experience virtually technically transparent to the common user. Furthermore, Linux does not offer nearly the array of polished applications that Windows does.

And yet Linux users say it is a far more stable, reliable system than Windows or Mac. Linux fans share stories of Linux-powered computers running for months and even years without crashing or needing to be rebooted. Linux is far more compact, less bloated than Windows, so it runs faster and requires a less powerful microprocessor.

And if your Linux system reveals a bug, you or any hacker* you know could conceivably fix it then and there, unlike a Microsoft system, for which you often need to wait days or weeks for a Microsoft employee to fix it for you. Computer users praise the robust stability of Linux, but they also praise the fact that you can make the program do exactly what you need it to do. If you have a quirky piece of hardware, you can customize Linux to made it work within your system

*Although among the civilian population the term *hacker* has come to hold a negative connotation—to conjure images of virus-writing, troublemaking, Pentagon-busting criminals—the word *hacker* is actually morally neutral. Used here and in the broad techie community, *hacker* simply means a programmer. To hack is to write computer code—any code, not just the kind that causes trouble. If anything, *hacker* is used among techies as a term of respect.

rather than wait and hope that Microsoft will come out with a product that might possibly sort of work.

So yes, Linux is good. It is more than good—by veteran users it is nothing short of beloved.

CHAPTER THREE

The Babbling Bazaar

How Linux Development Works

IN AN ARTICLE FOR *THE NEW YORK TIMES MAGAZINE*, WRITER AMY HARMON DESCRIBED A QUINTESSENTIAL MOMENT IN THE LIFE OF LINUX. MARCUS MEISSNER, AGE TWENTY-FIVE, OF ERLANGEN, GERMANY, WAS WORKING ON HIS HOME COMPUTER WHEN IT CRASHED. SO HE SENT OUT AN E-MAIL TO THE LARGER LINUX COMMUNITY. MOMENTS LATER HE GOT A PROPOSED FIX FROM A USER KNOWN AS MINGO, TWENTY-SIX, LIVING IN BUDAPEST, HUNGARY. SOON AFTER, PETKHAN, A BULGARIAN, SENT OVER ANOTHER PATCH. AS

Linus encourages feedback from Linux users.

Harmon writes, "The point was not simply to mend the program, but also to find the most elegant way of doing so. Of course everyone knew that Torvalds, the . . . spider at the center of this self-spinning web, would have the final say."

That's exactly how Linux works. Users put Linux through its paces in the course of their work or play, and when bugs turn up, they collaborate to fix them . . . *quickly*. In many cases, improvements to Linux come not just from debugging but from users adapting it to other uses—other kinds of microprocessors, for example, or new hardware devices, such as those used for voice recognition. As technology improves, Torvalds and his codevelopers seek to respond to each opportunity for Linux to become more useful, more efficient, and more cutting-edge.

What can you do if you want to get involved with Linux? Use it. When new Linux users ask Torvalds what they should work on, as they do hundreds of times a year, Torvalds tells them to use Linux and come back when they know the answer. "Just use the system, and you'll do Linux development because you want to."

Torvalds spends roughly eight to ten hours a day responding to e-mails, sorting through proposed patches, and writing some code himself. Though he writes a small fraction of the code now, he explains, "I'm the person with the global overview of what's going on in all the areas." He does not necessarily manage every part of the system. Under him is a second level of programmers who manage subsystems and send him patches that have already been vetted and cleaned up.

A true pragmatist, Torvalds does not like to set long-term goals for Linux but rather wants to remain open to new technological developments. "I intend to react to the marketplace and see what developers want to do."

Will Linux grow beyond a place that Torvalds can possibly control? Torvalds says no. Unlike most software masterminds, Torvalds is not interested in marketing, distribution, service, or customer support. He takes no responsibility for those massive efforts. He believes that if he and his fellow programmers can offer an excellent, stable, and ever-improving operating system, then they have done their job. The rest can take care of itself. "The good thing with technical pressures is that technical questions always have a good answer—it's only nontechnical questions that sometimes don't have an answer at all."

So Torvalds is concerned with the technical development of Linux and that alone. Therefore, he is grateful that money-making commercial ventures have swooped in to fill the needs he cannot and does not wish to fill. Does that mean companies are selling and profiting from Linux? Yes. We'll get to that in a minute.

Why Linux Development Works

In his enormously influential essay called *The Cathedral and the Bazaar*, programmer and open-source-code evangelist Eric Raymond tries to explain the strange and amazing psychology behind the Linux phenomenon. Linux employs no one, pays no one, and charges no one. It has no formal organization, no traditional distribution, no advertising, and no marketing. And yet its programmers are widely considered the best in the field, its adaptability and reliability are virtually unchallenged, and its rate of improvement is by far and away the best there is.

In his essay Raymond explains how the advent of Linux completely changed his notion of how really excellent software is created. Before Linux, Raymond was a devoted proponent of open-source development, but, he writes, "I believed that most important software . . . needed to be built like cathedrals, carefully crafted by individual wizards or small bands of mages [magicians] working in splendid isolation." He believed programmers needed to work and hone and rework until they could release something truly fine.

"Linus Torvalds's style of development—release early and often, delegate everything you can, be open to the point of promiscuity—came as a surprise," Raymond writes. "No quiet, reverent cathedral building here—rather the Linux community seemed to resemble a great babbling bazaar of differing agendas and approaches . . . out of which a coherent and stable system could seemingly emerge only by a succession of miracles."

But the Linux style *worked*. Raymond found that undeniable. "The Linux world not only didn't fly apart in confusion but seemed to go from strength to strength at a speed barely imaginable to cathedral builders."

Why?

Linux programmers, like Torvalds himself, are a self-selected group of people doing it for no other reason than they want to. For them, Raymond posits, it is intellectually stimulating to solve the specific problems they encounter in the most elegant way possible. It is gratifying to help create this instrument that is useful to them personally, free to all, and used by millions. It is professionally thrilling to collaborate with peers at such a high level of technical fluency and skill. Their work on Linux often makes a stark contrast to the way many of these programmers spend their days. "Too often," Raymond writes, "software developers spend their days grinding away for pay at programs they neither need nor love."

Because Linux developers are also Linux users, they are inherently familiar with the program and motivated to make it work well. Torvalds keeps his development crew busy and involved, constantly releasing new versions of the system and treating his developers as his most valuable resource. As Raymond describes, "Linus was keeping his hackers/users constantly stimulated and rewarded—stimulated by the prospect of having an ego-satisfying piece of the action, rewarded by the sight of constant (even *daily*) improvement in their work."

Because of the vast number of brains focusing on Linux, bugs make themselves apparent, and moreover, they become shallow and fixable. With all of those users, somebody will invariably find a problem, and somebody else will invariably come up with a patch to fix it. Often there will be many competing solutions, and Torvalds has the honor of deciding which code represents the best fix. How does he choose? The Linux community operates as a pure meritocracy. As Torvalds likes to say, "The best code wins." As respected a programmer as Torvalds is, he is equally respected for recognizing good programming from others.

Raymond cites the Internet as a necessary precondition for Linux. How else could Torvalds be in communication with thousands of code writers across the globe at the same time with whom he has no geographical, personal, or professional connection other than Linux? "Linux was the first project to make a conscious and successful effort to use the entire *world* as its talent pool. I don't think it's a coincidence that the gestation period of Linux coincided with the birth of the World Wide Web. . . . Linus was the first person who learned how to play by the new rules that pervasive Internet access made possible."

And finally, Raymond gives what is perhaps the most critical reason why the Linux process works: "We have *fun* doing what we do," Raymond explains. "Our creative play has been racking up technical, market-share, and mind-share successes at an astounding rate. We're proving not only that we can do better software, but that *joy is an asset*."

Torvalds heartily agrees. "The most important design issue . . . is that Linux is supposed to be fun."

The Larger Freeware Movement

Although Linux is probably the most famous and most celebrated open-source system, it is certainly not the only one. Apache, for example, is probably the most used application on the Internet, running over half of all web sites, including the big ones such as Yahoo! Apache is a freeware application developed by eight programmers with a common interest in server software. They began by passing around ideas, challenges, and solutions. They initially dubbed their software "A Patchy Server," jokingly referring to its ad hoc development style, but later renamed it Apache out of deference to the Native American tribe. Now even computer giant IBM has adopted Apache software, although the IBM legal department was puzzled to discover there was no one to whom they could pay a licensing fee. In return for use of the software, the loosely organized Apache Group requires only that their software be used nonexclusively—that the source code be available to anyone who wants it.

Sendmail, a freeware program originally created by Eric Allman, is responsible for routing more than 80 percent of the mail sent over the Internet. FreeBSD and NetBSD are, like Linux, free Unix-based operating systems, although unlike Linux, they have not maintained the same centralized control.

Netscape, the company that popularized the Internet with its Navigator browser, was so swayed by the arguments put forth by Eric Raymond in *The Cathedral and the Bazaar* that they released the browser's source code in March 1999. Fixes and adaptations came in from around the world, including a feature provided by a group of Australian programmers (within a few *hours* of Netscape releasing the code) that enabled secure transactions over the web. Within a month, Netscape had a new version of Navigator, ready to be downloaded.

The progress of freeware is so stunningly fast and effective, it is hard to imagine any individual or even corporation being able to match it. The Australians, mentioned above, did not get paid, but they commanded the attention and the respect of the worldwide programming community.

As journalist Josh McHugh wrote in his cover story for *Forbes* magazine, "Liberated software has become an intellectual Olympics, where some of the world's top engineering minds compete—not for venture capital, but for impressing their peers."

Although Torvalds has been a fantastically powerful and effective advocate for the open-source movement, he does not consider himself an idealist. Unlike the adherents of the Free Software Foundation, he does not consider himself political, either. For him, it is not about doing a good thing, although that is a very agreeable result. Open source, in his view, is the best, fastest, most pragmatic way to make great software. His primary objective is not that software be free but that it be excellent. And to be excellent, in his view, it needs to be free.

With the open-source movement rocketing ahead in efficiency and popularity, you have to wonder if it is starting to make the closed-source software giants a little nervous.

CHAPTER FOUR

The Big Time

Red Hat and Caldera Legitimize Linux for Corporate Use

THE REBELS OF LINUX ARE RAPIDLY GAINING CORPORATE LEGITIMACY WHETHER THEY LIKE IT OR NOT. RED HAT, A COMPANY BASED IN DURHAM, NORTH CAROLINA, WAS BEGUN BY A MAN NAMED MARC EWING IN ORDER TO PROVIDE SIMPLER, FRIENDLIER ACCESS TO LINUX. HE KNEW THAT LINUX COULDN'T OFFER THE KIND OF PACKAGING AND CUSTOMER SUPPORT THAT WOULD GIVE LINUX A SERIOUS FOOTHOLD IN THE BUSINESS AND DESKTOP MARKETS. BIG CORPORATIONS

Executives from Red Hat Software, a company that provides access to Linux services

feared Linux for the same reason so many techies love it—nobody owns it. Because nobody owns it, corporations assumed they would have no recourse if it stopped working—nobody to help them get it running again, nobody to sue, nobody from whom they could withhold payment.

Ewing started Red Hat to provide these very services, including instruction manuals and telephone support. Individual users often want a more polished-looking desktop and a simpler interface than they find in the raw downloads of Linux, and Red Hat offers that, too. For about $50, Red Hat will provide you with a CD offering easy installation of Linux (a process that can otherwise be famously thorny) as well as several handy applications geared for desktop use.

Many veterans questioned the wisdom of Red Hat trying to sell something anybody can get for free, but a few big players thought Ewing was making a very smart move. Substantial investments in Red Hat came from Intel, the gargantuan chip maker, and Netscape. Red Hat stays true to the spirit of Linux in some respects—any code it adds to Linux, it releases under open-source rules. In other respects they do not—they want and need to make money. Lots of it, preferably. Red Hat is now a publicly traded company on the stock market worth several billion dollars.

Caldera Systems is another company distributing Linux and offering corporate training and support. As with Red Hat, they make it clear that they are not charging money for intellectual property. They are charging money for services to support that intellectual property.

How does Torvalds feel about this?

"The commercial vendors are good, yes. They all use the standard kernel, so technically there's not much to worry about. And they tend to position the systems around Linux differently to target different markets. I couldn't do that even if I wanted to, and I don't want to," he says. "There [is] such a synergy between having commercial people who wanted to make it easy to install and technical people who wanted to do the right thing technically that I'm not worried anymore. . . . I just don't see how we can lose."

Commercial vendors such as Red Hat and Caldera have given Linux an enormous lift in the market. Now hardware vendors such as IBM, Dell Computer, Corel Computer, and VA Research are offering computers with Linux preinstalled.

Developers have adapted a version of Linux for the handheld PalmPilot.

More and more, computer buyers will have a choice—they will not be forced to buy a PC preequipped with Microsoft; they will be able to choose Linux. Gigantically successful technology companies such as Oracle and Sun Microsystems are writing versions of their software to run on Linux. Now application buyers, too, will have a choice of operating systems on which they would like to run the application, and Linux will be among the options. A version of Linux has been ported to the handheld PalmPilot. Even a few of the world's most popular games such as Quake and Doom have been ported to Linux. After two decades of a near monopoly for Microsoft, this is a dream come true for Torvalds and his code-writing cohorts—and for virtually every proponent of open source.

Now corporate America is turning to Linux as well. Go.com, the online division of Disney, switched to Linux. Weather.com turned to Linux as well. SBC Communications installed it on thirty-six desktop computers. "And now," says technical manager Randy Kessel, "we spend a tenth of the administration cost for those desktops that we do for the rest." Digital Domain, the special-effects company owned by movie-producer James Cameron, chose Linux to run the computers on which they created the special effects for *Titanic*.

Archive Retrieval, an electronic-document-retrieval company, installed a system for the city of Medina, Washington, on computers running Linux. Ray A. Jones, president, remembers when a bug was revealed in Medina's new system. "We asked a question on the Internet, and within a couple of hours we had an answer," he said. "I fixed it myself with three lines of code. With a commercial product I'd have had to wait for Microsoft to fix it—if it ever did. This way, the whole Linux community benefited." In an ironic twist, the city of Medina adopted the system in part because of the four filing cabinets jammed with documents concerning the mansion constructed by Bill Gates.

The U.S. government has come to rely on Linux as well. NASA used Linux as the basis of a computer cluster that is among the five hundred fastest computer systems in the world and saved 90 percent of the cost of what a similarly fast supercomputer would have been. Los Alamos National Laboratory researchers hooked up sixty-eight computers running Linux to function as a single supercomputer and reached a speed of

Linux helped NASA to develop one of the fastest computer systems in the world.

19 billion calculations per second. That ranks it as the 315th fastest computer in the world. It has been running for three months and has not had to be rebooted once. The Oak Ridge National Laboratory uses Linux as well.

Linux has undeniably become a legitimate player in the world of computers. Its use is growing at an estimated 40 percent a year. It is fast, powerful, flexible, and free. Which brings us to the question . . .

Is Bill Gates Scared?

Well, yes and no. It is hard to say just how serious a threat Linux is to the all-powerful Microsoft Windows. To put things in perspective, last year roughly 9 million computers were running Linux and roughly 300 million were running Microsoft Windows. Windows tends to run on 90 to 95 percent of the world's desktop computers. All the other operating systems—MacOS, Linux, Unix, Sun, and several others—share that remaining 5 to 10 percent. In a nutshell, Microsoft is *huge*. But you probably already knew that.

What counts in the business world is not so much size but trend. Financial analysts want to know whether your market share is growing or declining. That is the critical question. That is what shareholders care about. That is what keeps computer executives tossing and turning at night. Are you coming or are you going?

Linux is definitely coming. But is Microsoft going?

TECH TALK

What Is Open-Source Code?

You may have heard of a thing called *open-source code*. What exactly is open-source code, and why is it starting to become so famous?

When a company or a person writes a computer program and gives that program's source code to anyone who wants it, the code is referred to as *open source*. A programmer who writes open-source programs is much like a master chef who invents new recipes and then publishes them in the newspaper.

What is source code? Programmers write their programs in high-level computer languages like C++, Java, or Smalltalk. The program written in the high-level language is known as the *source code*. Next, the source code is translated into *machine language* so that the computer can run it. Machine language is just a series of zeroes and ones, called *binary*, that the computer can understand. Computers cannot understand high-level languages directly, and people find it very difficult to read machine language, so it always needs to be translated.

For example, if I wanted to tell the computer to print the word "hello," the instructions in a high-level language might look like this:

printf("hello");

After being changed into binary, the instructions might look like this:

1010000101011101101001010101010100101010100010101010

Although the computer itself can read the machine language, in order for a programmer to easily understand what the computer is really doing, she needs to see the program before it has been translated. In other words, the programmer needs to have the source code.

Many companies (like Microsoft) literally lock the source code for their programs away, because they feel that if the code fell into other people's hands, their ideas might be stolen and they might lose money.

Open source is a powerful idea because, instead of locking the code away, the code's developer allows the entire community of programmers to use it and improve on it. Also, if a bug is discovered in the code, it is likely to be fixed more quickly than it might if only the original developers were allowed to work on it.

For example, let's say I were to write a word-processing program for the Macintosh. Now, let's say another developer was also writing a word-processing program for the Macintosh. If my program was not open source, we would both do the same work and we might end up with very similar products. But in the open-source world, the second developer would start with my source code and then, perhaps, spend all of her time adding a complex spell checker. She would then give me back the updated source, and we would both end up with a product that was better then either of us would have made alone.

Some people believe that Microsoft is too huge *not* to keep winning. It is the beneficiary of a whirling virtual circle. Too many individuals and companies depend on it. The worlds of software and hardware are all built around Microsoft. It is hard to budge a product so well established.

Others believe that Microsoft is indeed vulnerable. First and most important because many people, including Torvalds, feel that while many of Microsoft's software applications are adequate or even good, its operating system, the linchpin of its success, is basically bad. According to Torvalds: "Microsoft has been very much into making the user interface look good, but internally it's just a complete mess. And even people who program for Microsoft and who have had years of experience just don't know how it works internally. Worse, nobody dares change it. Nobody dares to fix bugs because it's such a mess that fixing one bug might just break a hundred programs that depend on that bug. And Microsoft isn't interested in anyone fixing bugs—they're interested in making money."

Does Bill Gates see Linux as a potential threat?

Many of the open-source proponents believe that Microsoft is being left in the dust by the lightning-fast improvements of open-source projects such as Linux. Microsoft releases new versions of Windows roughly every three years—nothing like the speed of Linux. And Microsoft, although it certainly employs many gifted programmers, simply can't compete with the thousands—even millions—committing brainpower to Linux. Besides that, Linux proponents believe users will become impatient with the inaccessibility of Microsoft's source code. Robert Young, Red Hat's chief executive, compared buying closed-source software to buying a car with its hood welded shut.

Another potential threat to Microsoft is security, a paramount issue since the explosion of the Internet. Devastating viruses have been launched through Microsoft's popular Outlook e-mail application. Writer Patrick Humphreys described it this way: "In the 1990s the world's computing stock became a monoculture, like a forest with just one type of tree. Any disease can decimate it."

Is Linux more secure? Torvalds thinks so. "If you look at security bulletins, Linux is impacted by security bugs as much as any other vendor. The thing is that when you get the bulletin, Linux already has a patch for it, while the other vendors tend to say, 'We are investigating.' "

Microsoft also has to fear something called WINE. WINE is a Windows emulator, a software program written by Linux developers to enable Linux to run all software applications written for Windows. Although WINE is already up and running, it is not yet as polished and reliable as Torvalds would like. He and his fellow programmers expect it will be soon and that once it is, WINE could dramatically erode Microsoft's competitive edge.

Is Microsoft aware of these potential threats? Yes. An internal Microsoft memo was leaked to the outside world, making it clear that Microsoft is aware of what they are up against. The memo states: "Linux and other O.S.S. [open-source systems] advocates are making a progressively more credible argument that O.S.S. software is at least as robust—if not more—than commercial alternatives. . . . The ability of the O.S.S. process to collect and harness the collective IQ of thousands of individuals across the Internet is simply amazing."

So, yes. Bill Gates is probably at least a little scared. He is certainly aware of Linux and its heralded creator, although he and Torvalds definitely do not travel in the same circles.

Asked whether he had ever met Bill Gates in person, Torvalds responded, "I have never met him, and I suspect we won't have that much to talk about. We may both have operating systems, but he is a marketing guy, and I am a technical guy."

Asked whether he believes the fear of Linux is keeping Bill Gates awake at night, Torvalds thinks probably not. "I don't know. . . . I don't think they're *really* nervous. I think they [Microsoft] are mildly nervous. I don't think Bill Gates spends the nights lying there thinking about Linux."

Torvalds may be right about Bill Gates not spending his nights thinking about Linux. But according to a recent report on the future of open source, maybe Gates should be.

This is what lines of computer code actually look like!

The Future of Open Source

According to a report issued in 2000 by Forrester Research, Linux and other open-source projects will completely change the software landscape by the year 2004. "Proprietary software vendors will suddenly see software development as an unfair fight: their mercenary band of captive developers against a battalion of Internet-armed revolutionaries," the report predicts. It concludes that all software vendors will be forced to open their code or substantially lower the price of their licenses.

The report, titled "Open Source Cracks the Code," was compiled from interviews of information technology (IT) managers at 2,500 companies. The report found that 56 percent of the companies were already using open-source software.

It predicts among the winners will be IBM, which it calls the "Infrastructure Gorilla" because it already offers and supports open-source systems, and Dell Computer because it, too, seems to be offering strong support to open-source software such as Linux.

And the losers? The big one, not surprisingly, is Microsoft. Forrester Research predicts that Microsoft's corporate culture and strategy contrast so strikingly with the open-source model that it will begin to fade, eventually surviving only as what is called a "legacy vendor," hanging around to support its old products.

Needless to say, Linux fans were pleased with the report. "Ha!" said George Nobick, a Linux developer. "Microsoft may own the desktop now, but we own the future."

Is Torvalds hoping that Linux will replace Microsoft as the world's software powerhouse? Not at all. "I'm actually hoping that it won't take more than 25 or 30 percent of the market. If Linux owned 95 percent of the market, it would be equally as sick. There is some need for competition."

While there are strong arguments to be made against Microsoft, many people believe that Microsoft will remain a formidable software power well into the future. In any case, Bill Gates would do well to consider that penguins aren't always cute and cuddly. They do bite.

Transmeta

In December 1996, Torvalds went from living what was possibly the least-secretive professional life in the world of computing to the most secretive. One week after their first child, Patricia Miranda Torvalds, was born, the happy parents moved their little family from Helsinki, Finland, to Santa Clara, California. Santa Clara is right smack in the middle of the fabled Silicon Valley, the historical hotbed of high tech. They moved into a modest tract house (featuring lots of stuffed penguins), and Torvalds signed on as a programmer at a company called Transmeta. His first so-called real job.

What does Transmeta do? It is a good question that until recently had no answer. Transmeta kept their mission so secret that no employee was allowed to speak a word about what they were doing. Transmeta's office kept their windows darkened. They would not even say when they were likely to say anything about what they were working on. Rumors abounded, and the hire of Linus Torvalds only fanned the flames of curiosity.

Transmeta became the biggest mystery in Silicon Valley. "I could tell you what I'm working on, but then I'd have to kill you," Torvalds joked if anyone asked him about his new job.

Although people questioned why Torvalds remained in Finland as long as he did, Torvalds is quick to praise his mother country. "One major advantage of being from Finland was the very high level of education (and it was pretty much free, so I didn't have to worry about economic issues when getting an education). And the fact that Finland is very high tech—I think Finland is number one in the world when it comes to the number of Internet accesses per person." There is another way in which his homeland fundamentally shaped his life: "In Finland, the worth of a person isn't measured in dollars," he says.

Still, he is certainly appreciative of the benefits of his new home in California. "I like the weather a lot. . . . I don't remember the last time I couldn't walk around in shorts all day." He also finds the level of high-tech activity in the legendary Silicon Valley stimulating. "While Finland was very high-tech, Finnish companies tend to be very traditional and

Torvalds demonstrates the new Crusoe chip.

not taking many risks and doing the really interesting stuff. Silicon Valley is completely different: people here really live on the edge, and there are lots of very technically interesting projects here."

Transmeta has turned out to be one of those interesting projects. In January 2000, the company finally broke its silence, announcing its plan for a groundbreaking new microchip called the Crusoe. The Crusoe is meant to run virtually any operating system or application by tricking the

Linus Torvalds and Dave Ditzel, CEO of Transmeta Corp., present Crusoe chips.

software into thinking it is running on one of Intel's ubiquitous chips built on the x86 architecture—the same architecture that Torvalds first designed Linux around. The Crusoe chip does not use the x86 architecture; it uses something called VLIW, or Very Long Instruction Word. So how does Crusoe trick the software? With what the programmers at Transmeta call code-morphing software. Code-morphing software sits not on top of the operating system, as software applications always have, but *under* the operating system. "The OS thinks it's running on a bare piece of hardware," Torvalds explains.

This extra layer of software actually does a lot of the processing work that the chip typically has to do, and that means the Crusoe chip needs many fewer transistors. This in turn means that Crusoe can work in more compact systems—such as handheld computers and Internet phones, the kinds of devices that experts believe will account for much of the computer market in the future. Another benefit is that the extra layer of software makes Crusoe easily, almost instantly, upgradable. These features could likely make the Crusoe chip,

Linus Torvalds looks toward a bright future.

once it is produced, a serious threat to Intel.

Torvalds was recruited by Transmeta to help design and write this code-morphing software. David Ditzel, Transmeta's founder, wanted Torvalds not for his Linux fame—which was considerably smaller at the end of 1996 than it is today—but for his excellent programming abilities and his deep familiarity with the x86 chip structure. Torvalds, for his part, felt that "Transmeta was doing something that nobody else was doing." Torvalds was also gratified that Transmeta was already using Linux and that they agreed to his spending a certain portion of his time continuing to work on Linux. This came as welcome news to Linux users as well. Torvalds consciously decided against working for one of the commercial Linux vendors because he did not want to be pulled from the technical side of his work, and he did not want to show preferential treatment to any single vendor.

It is worth noting that the principal investor in Transmeta is none other than Paul Allen, cofounder of Microsoft and former partner of Bill Gates.

A Satisfying Life

Torvalds undoubtedly has his hands full with his exciting, demanding job at Transmeta and the oversight of Linux. He is in heavy demand at computer conferences and expos around the globe and throughout the year. In addition, he makes time spent with his wife, Tove, and their two young daughters, Patricia and Daniela, a top priority in his life. A journalist named Charles Babcock described the following scene at the Open Source in Business Forum at Stanford University: "Torvalds's wife, Tove, arranged herself and their blond children on the floor before the front row. Halfway through the proceedings the youngest Torvalds let out a cry . . . and Linus casually exited the panel to help rearrange his family in a more distant part of the hall. No one considered this unusual because the Torvalds treated it as part of everyday life." Although he is famous and beloved in his field, he lives a modest, unassuming life, as evidenced by the plain green Pontiac he drives.

Torvalds does not have a jet, and he has no plans to buy one, but he has derived immense pleasure from the technical achievement of Linux, not to mention all the acclaim it has won him and his codevelopers. In 1999 he was named Person of the Year by *PC Magazine* and given the Award for Industry Achievement by *InfoWorld Magazine*.

For Torvalds, ultimately it is not about money, and it is not about stuff, and it is not about a big, fancy office. As one developer put it, "For engineers, it's all about the cool hack." And Torvalds is the master of the cool hack. He has created a living, thriving community out of the cool hack.

In a live online chat on the television channel MSNBC, a Linux user asked Torvalds if he had ever tried to figure out how much money he could have made from licensing Linux. Torvalds responded, "I haven't even tried. I know how much fun I've had."

sources and bibliography

Raymond, Eric. *The Cathedral and the Bazaar*. New York: O'Reilly and Associates, 1999.

Wayner, Peter. *Free for All: How LINUX and The Free Software Movement Undercut the High-Tech Titans*. New York: HarperBusiness, 2000.

Young, Robert, and Wendy Goldman Rohm. *How Red Hat Changed the Software Business and Took Microsoft by Surprise*. Scottsdale: The Coriolis Group, 1999.

The following magazines and online services were also used:

Forbes	www.bootnet.com
Linux Magazine	www.linuxjournal.com
The New York Times	www.linuxworld.com
San Jose Mercury News	www.msnbc.com
Time	www.virtualfinland.com
USA Today	www.wired.com
Wired	www.zdnet.com

index

Page numbers in *italics* refer to illustrations.

Photography credits